THE
FEAR
BOOK

FACING FEAR ONCE AND FOR ALL

CHERI HUBER

Special thanks to:

Monique and Brian

All who have faced the fear
and all who will

Books by Cheri Huber and Ashwini Narayanan

Published by Keep It Simple Books

Making a Change for Good: A Guide to Compassionate Self-Discipline

Don't Suffer, Communicate! A Zen Guide to Compassionate Communication

The Big Bamboozle: How You Get Conned Out of the Life You Want and What to Do about It

What Universe Are You Creating? Zen and the Art of Recording and Listening

I Don't Want To, I Don't Feel Like It: How Resistance Controls Your Life and What to Do about It

Books by Cheri Huber

There Is Nothing Wrong with You: Going Beyond Self-Hate

What You Practice Is What You Have: A Guide to Having the Life You Want

The Fear Book: Facing Fear Once and for All, Rev. Ed.

The Depression Book: Depression as an Opportunity for Spiritual Growth, Expanded and Revised

Transform Your Life: A Year of Awareness Practice

The Key and the Name of the Key Is Willingness

Be the Person You Want to Find: Relationship and Self-Discovery

How You Do Anything Is How You Do Everything, Rev. Ed.

Suffering Is Optional: Three Keys to Freedom and Joy

When You're Falling, Dive: Acceptance, Possibility and Freedom

Nothing Happens Next: Responses to Questions about Meditation

Trying to Be Human: Zen Talks

Sweet Zen: Dharma Talks with Cheri Huber

There Are No Secrets: Zen Meditation with Cheri Huber (DVD)

Unconditional Self-Acceptance: A Do-It-Yourself Course on CD
Published by Sounds True

How to Get from Where You Are to Where You Want to Be
Published by Hay House

Table of Contents

WHAT FEAR IS

In the process presented here for dealing with fear, fear is the hunted, not the hunter. Fear is the quarry you must stalk and confront and unmask to reveal that all that separates you from yourself is an illusion.

Fear is not what you think it is.

Fear is not who you are at your core. Fear is not the real you that you must somehow fix or improve or overcome.

Fear is a very useful signal along the path to freedom. The stronger the fear, the closer you are to what you are seeking. If you want to stay "safe" (stuck where you are), fear tells you to stop what you are doing. But if you want to be free, fear lets you know you are on the right track;

it is a signal to push ahead in the same direction, to pick up the pace.

Student and Guide: Overeating

Student: I think that I am not a fearful person. Fear just isn't much of an issue in my life. And I don't see much connection between fear and what is a serious issue for me, overeating.

Guide: You could go somewhere where eating is taken out of your hands, and you could see a lot of things about it.

Student: Well, that I can't choose when and what I am going to eat is one thing that keeps me from going on retreat.

Guide: That is fear. Some of the things we may not think of as fear—anger, sadness, irritation, urgency, depression, control issues—are pointing to underlying fear. So if you hear yourself say you don't like not getting to decide what and when you eat, look underneath that and see if there is some panic about not being in charge.

Resistance is one of the processes that mask fear.

"I don't enjoy

swimming/dancing/parties/
cities/camping/group
discussions/traveling..."

"I'm not interested. It's not my kind of thing."

"I've done that already and don't need to prove anything by doing it again."

"I would love to, but I tried and I just can't."

"I'm taking care of myself by staying away from this thing I'm not ready for."

"I'm not afraid, I just don't want to."

"It's dangerous."

"It's silly."

"It's boring."

Every time we choose "safety," we reinforce fear.

When we try to avoid the discomfort we call fear, our world grows smaller and smaller.

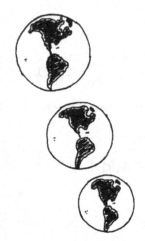

We find ways to avoid
   people
   activities
   circumstances
   experiences
that might cause us to have the reaction
we fear.

As we grow older, we become afraid of
more and more.

Then we close down.
We close off.
And our lives shrink.

When we attempt something new and find ourselves feeling really uncomfortable, we believe the discomfort means that something is wrong, so we try to get out of the situation.

As time goes on, we learn to get out sooner and sooner, until we move directly to avoidance, even before we consider doing something that might be scary.

Can you list the things you used to enjoy that you no longer do because they are too scary?

- DRIVING ON FREEWAYS
- MAKING NEW FRIENDS
- TAKING RISKS

However, there are things,
like falling in love,
that we do precisely because they leave
us sweaty of palm,
short of breath,
and weak of knee.

A lot of advertising promises that same
breathless thrill. Go there, buy this, wear
this, and then
you'll feel
that way.

The irony is that even when we pursue
those desirable feelings,

our world still shrinks!

Whether we are:

avoiding all that could produce the
dreaded discomfort we call fear, or

pursuing all that could produce the
desirable feeling we call excitement,

we are removed from the present
moment by the belief that our lives
will be the way they should be only in

some other time,
some other place,
some other alternative
      to what is
                  here
                        and
                              now.

The relentless pursuit of happiness
is one definition of suffering.

The single-minded avoidance of pain
is another.

I knew a woman who was convinced that
her happiness depended on marrying a
wealthy man. Nothing in life interested
her except wealthy men, and her world
became small and exceedingly unhappy.

Our world shrinks when we are paralyzed
by fear of making mistakes
and by fear of doing something wrong.

But if we simply take a step and see what
happens, our world
opens a little bit.

Then we can take
another step.

Every step enlarges
our view; everything
we do shows us
something.

As the old Zen masters say,
when we are willing
to pay attention,
everything enlightens us.

A friend used to say to me:

"I'm afraid I'm not going to get a job."
"I'm afraid of being alone."
"I'm afraid I'll run out of money."

The list went on and on. I would try to help her address each fear until I realized that we were dealing with problems that did not exist.

The constant was "I'm afraid," which could be followed by an endless series of purely imaginary difficulties.

Only when we focused
on the <u>process</u>
rather than the <u>content</u>
could we begin to address
what was really going on.

We could talk for
hours,
days,
lifetimes
about what is wrong,
what could happen,
what won't work.

Don't do it.

Instead, take a step. Look around, see
where you are, and see what your next
step will be. Take that step, see where
you are, and the next step becomes
clear. Maybe it's back to where you
started.

You cannot know until you get there. Each
step is clear only from where you are at
the moment. The final step is not
apparent at the beginning, only from the
step immediately before it.

Each step is part of a learning process, and since no matter what you do you will learn something,

**there is no way
to make a mistake.**

**There is simply no reason
to be afraid.**

Sitting around
thinking about what
won't work is like a
scientist deciding the
result of an
experiment
beforehand—not a
way to learn anything.

If we really want to know how something
is, or what is possible, we plunge ahead.

We might not find what we thought we
would find,

but we will find something.

Life is a creative process, and creativity has to have that WHOLEHEARTED ABANDON of PLUNGING AHEAD, taking the next step in the knowledge that we will learn something.

It is not possible to make a mistake.
We cling to the idea
of making a mistake
to maintain the delusion
that we can know
what cannot possibly be known:
what hasn't happened yet.

Fear of Fear: The Sensations of Fear

Several years ago while visiting my daughter and my first grandchild, who was then a toddler, I decided to build a fence around the backyard so my grandson could play freely and safely outside. I had only a few days for the project, my daughter had no tools or supplies, and it was summer in Georgia (90 degrees Fahrenheit and 90% humidity) so I knew it would be a challenge. But I also knew I would rest easier 3000 miles away at home if I could picture Brian with a secure play area.

I began early and worked late.

We made frequent trips in their little car for boards, posthole diggers, and dozens of things I hadn't considered before I took on the task. And we had fun with everyone, including Brian, helping out.

The last evening before my flight home, we made the big push to finish. By working until dark (about 9:00 p.m.) and a few hours the next morning, I figured I just might finish. We had to go into town for a couple of last-minute items, and to save time we had a fast-food dinner.

By 10:00 p.m. everyone was in bed. I was having a cup of tea when I began

to feel anxious. My first thought was that perhaps there was someone outside the house; maybe I'd heard a noise and was responding to it even though it hadn't consciously registered. I peered out of every window, closed the curtains, turned on the exterior lights, and went back to my tea. The anxiety grew.

I could feel that I was headed for what is called a panic attack. My brain was searching, scanning, scrambling frantically to figure out the cause of this momentary hysteria. I was covered in a cold sweat, my heart was pounding, my breath was approaching a pant. I tried to focus my awareness on breathing to calm my body down.

"What is this? What's wrong?" I asked myself. "If this is a premonition, then we are very near the end. The missiles must be on their way. No, that's crazy. But what is it? Am I worried I won't get the fence finished? Ridiculous! I could always postpone the flight. Am I worried the plane will crash? That's not it. What is it?" In a few minutes, I was in the bathroom, as sick as I had ever been. Dinner exploded from my body. Finally, it came to me. I had food poisoning.

My stomach was churning; my mind was racing; I was cold, clammy, and weak. Since I had never been poisoned before, my mind had no experience of this, and so it went to the only thing it knew could explain the sensations. "This is fear. Something awful must be about to happen." But those sensations had nothing to do with fear. The sensations were my body trying to expel poison. Not only did my explanation to myself not prevent something from happening, i.e., getting sick, but by focusing on something purely imaginary, it took my attention away from what was actually happening.

*****

Here's a common question:
Without fear,
wouldn't you just walk out into traffic?

The belief is that being afraid keeps you from doing something dangerous or just dumb. But that's one of the processes fear uses to protect itself.

When we look more closely we begin to see, especially if we decide to approach something we are afraid of, that fear is protecting itself against us.

It looks as if fear
is on your side,
taking care of you,
keeping you safe,

UNTIL YOU DECIDE TO DO SOMETHING IT TELLS YOU NOT TO DO!

At that point you become enemies. You are in an adversarial relationship with that which supposedly is protecting you.

In other words, rather than simply being a signal that something is going on, fear begins to look like an active force with an agenda of its own.

One might conclude that fear itself is the danger.

You are home alone. It is the middle of the night. A sound from another room wakes you. You lie in bed with your mind scrambling for an explanation. Nothing fits except someone has entered the house.

Your stomach is knotted,
your palms are sweaty,
your breath is shallow,
your heart knocks in your chest.

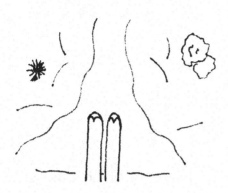

You are at the top of a ski slope. You look down and what you see is steep and icy.

Your heart pounds,
your breath is shallow,
your stomach is in knots
you break into a cold sweat.

THREE

Early evening and you have cooked dinner
for someone you recently met, someone
who just might turn out to be the most
wonderful person in the world. This is the
very person that all your life you've been
waiting to meet. It's fifteen minutes
before your guest arrives. As you make
a final check of the house, the meal, and
your appearance,

your palms are clammy,
your stomach tightens,
your breathing quickens,
your heart....

Three very different situations.

First, a prowler in your house, which could be life-threatening

Second, physical activity you have not only chosen but have paid a lot of money to do

Third, an emotional experience you have dreamed of and wished for

The physiological responses are very similar in each case, but how we think and feel about the situation—whether it is acceptable or not—determines whether we label the experience "fear." In the case of the potential romance, we might call the experience excited anticipation; on the ski slope, it could be exhilaration or thrill; hearing a prowler, we might call it terror.

If we can simply be with whatever is being experienced, there is no problem.

29

shallow breath
pounding heart
tight stomach
sweaty palms

These sensations do not mean that you should or should not do anything.

They don't mean anything at all.

But when we feel threatened, we believe those sensations mean something terrible is going to happen to us, something that we cannot stand, and we extend that to mean we will die.

In fact, nothing has happened to us that we did not survive.

The fear of fear
shrinks our world.

We will do anything to avoid the
discomfort of fear, even though we have

<u>never</u> examined
the experience itself,

<u>never</u> looked to see
exactly what it is,

<u>never</u> considered that it
might not mean what we think it means.

The Emptiness of Fear

Much of what we call fear is thought.

For example, a car swerves in front of you and everything goes into slow motion. Adrenaline rushes through the body at the moment of danger, and evasive actions are taken to avoid a collision. In that moment, there are no thoughts, just a oneness with the situation. Instead of thinking about what to do, there is just doing the next thing.

Many people report that in situations when they are truly threatened, there is no fear. The whole experience arises in each moment—there's turning the wheel of the car, there's stepping on the brake—but there is no experience of anyone doing it, of making conscious decisions.

I consider this phenomenon some of our
best evidence that fear
does not help us,
does not protect us,
does not take care of us.

"Fear" comes in afterwards.

Only later are there thoughts of what
might have happened.

"The car almost hit us."
"Another few yards and we would have
gone off the road."
"I could have been killed."

In fact, none of these things happened.
All that happened was sensations and
thoughts about those sensations.

**What most of us think of as fear
is primarily a mental process
of imagining situations
that do not exist in the moment.**

WHERE FEAR COMES FROM

Student and Guide: The Dinner Party

Student: I am going to a dinner party with some people I don't know very well, and I'm worried that my hands will shake like they always have at times like these. I know this could be an opportunity to be compassionate with myself whether I'm shaking or not. But I say maybe not yet, maybe not with these people. I go back and forth with it. I think I'll go. No, maybe I'll take one of my pills so I won't shake.

Guide: Do you consider going and shaking?

Student: And just not eating the soup? "Don't serve me soup, please."

Guide: You are trying to avoid an experience that could be helpful for you. What if you turned this around? What about going with an attitude of...

Student: Hoping they serve the soup?

Guide: Yes, and telling yourself this could be really interesting. Otherwise, the underlying message is that other people are more important than you are. For the part of you who is afraid, it's one more bit of information that what other people think is more important than her feelings. No wonder she is afraid.

Conditioning

How has it happened that
we live much of our adult
lives in a straitjacket of
fear?

Children don't know there is anything to
be afraid of. Up until around age five or
six, children are not particularly self-
conscious, they aren't awkward, they
don't think in terms of something being
wrong with them.

There was a time for each of us when we
were confident and capable and open and
eager to learn to do new things. In the
process of being socialized, that was
destroyed. We were taught to leave
ourselves and focus on others, and we
were warned and
cautioned and
threatened into near paralysis.

We had little support from adults for our
confidence and
capabilities and
eagerness to learn and explore
because they never had
that support themselves.

We grew to feel inadequate and insecure
and anxious, and by projecting that onto
our own children
we pass along the fear.

To make the transition
from our early sense
of fearlessness
and complete adequacy
to live freely
and function well in the world,
we needed support
we did not get.

Instead, we were given
the assumption that **fear**
is what keeps us safe.

In fact, **intelligence**
is what keeps us safe.

At the age when most kids learn to ride a bicycle, safety isn't really an issue for them. They aren't yet thinking there's any danger because they're not clinging to life the way we have learned to. They don't look at activities from the point of view of what terrible thing might happen. Little kids don't imagine that they might spend the rest of their lives in a wheelchair.

But a child who wants to learn to ride a bicycle can't get the simple information he or she needs without big doses of other stuff: how they're not doing it right and what could happen if they do it wrong.

All of this comes at a child in a way that is hard to grasp, except for the message

there is something
to be afraid of.

The child doesn't know exactly what that is but can hardly avoid concluding that his or her lack of adequacy is part of the problem. After receiving so much of that kind of information, a child simply won't try new things that bring up those feelings. It is just too scary.

Instead of that kind of information, what if the child is taught to ride the bicycle without all the warnings and threats and anxiety, not assuming he or she should already know that streets are dangerous or how to handle a bike around cars, dogs, kids, other bikers? (How would a little kid know all this?) What would be helpful is for someone to explain it all, the subtleties and nuances, not as if the child is stupid or careless or headed for disaster, but by way of giving information to someone who doesn't have it.

(Notice how commonly the information is passed on with an attitude of disdain, with the implication of someone's inadequacy, in a tone of voice that says, "What's the matter with you that you didn't already know that?" That's how we were spoken to as children, and we are mostly unaware of such subtle put-downs when we speak this way to others.)

Another way of describing what happens to children is that they're going along completely involved in their experience of the moment, with no illusion of being separate from anything, when somebody yells at them that they've done something wrong.

STOP
THAT
RIGHT
NOW!

They're jolted out of their natural ease and confidence and plunged into the awful energy of an adult's anger and fear. Suddenly, they're being told they've done something wrong and are yanked away from their own experience into a nightmare of confusion. The underlying message is that paying attention to ourselves, to our own world experience, is wrong and that to be safe we must give our attention to others.

This happens again and again, until we have our own repertoire of voices cautioning us and warning us and

threatening us, reinforcing the idea that we cannot be trusted with ourselves.
"You should've known better."
"What's the matter with you? Can't you do anything right?"
"This is too hard for you."

And now as adults we replay those messages to ourselves internally, undermining our own adequacy.

What we need for that transition from the innocent mind and heart of the child to an adult who can function well in the world is someone who knows the ropes, who can tell us how things work, who can guide us lovingly from not knowing to becoming capable and confident with whatever arises.

For most of us, as we were growing up that is what was missing in our lives.

Student and Guide: Fear of Failure

Student: Here's one. I sit down to work and fear comes up.
"What if it's no good?
What if I can't do it?"

Guide: Well, let's suppose you sat down to work and I walked up and said, "What if that's no good? What if you can't do it?"

Student: Hmmm. I think I'd wonder why you were saying that. I think it would make me mad. Who do you think you are, questioning my ability?

Guide: Okay. If someone "outside" of you expresses a belief in your inadequacy, it would make you question their motivation; it would make you angry that they would even think such a thing. But if someone "inside" you expresses the same belief in your inadequacy, you go to what you call fear.

Student: That sounds like it.

Guide: Good. Now where in that is the fear? Even if you are not successful with what you're working on, do you believe the result will be humiliation? Will you suffer rejection? Will you wind up on the street living out of a shopping cart? Will you not survive? What is going on?

Student: I don't know. I just know that when that voice suggests that I'm going to fail, it's like an icy hand grasps my heart.

Guide: And that's the "fear" that rules our lives. Someone says something that implies something is going to happen to me in some future time and place, my body is filled with sensations, and I'm conditioned to believe that means

something about who I am,
that I should do something,
that I should not do something,
that there is something wrong,
that I'm in big trouble.

That's a lot of being jerked around by
one little voice asking one little question.
But if we never examine it closely enough
to see that it's a conditioned voice
programmed to ask anxiety producing
questions, we would remain convinced
that it is the voice of God threatening us
with imminent destruction.

Spiritually, it is essential to understand
that there is nothing
in fear that is helping us.

Someone who lives at another Zen
Center was telling me how she spent last
winter in terror because she was getting
close to dropping everything and being in
the moment. She would get right to that

point, she could see that being in the moment was freedom, and all that was there was terror.

Now, what is that TERROR?

It is egocentricity
losing its grip on you.

You were taught that
fear is useful,
that it takes care of you.

When you begin to let go of it,
a part of you feels like it is dying,
and it doesn't want to die.

It would rather you died.
It would rather your world shrank
until there was nothing left of you.

But if you no longer believe
what fear tells you,
you will live
and it will not.
That is the point on the spiritual journey
that

almost nobody gets past.

When that TERROR arises,
when it gets backed into a corner,
when it is a matter of its survival
or yours,
almost nobody has the required
combination of
courage, desperation, willingness...
to stand up to it.

When this force in you that has controlled
and motivated you all your life is
screaming,

"If you do that
you're going to die!"

very few people are going to say, "Well, I just need to find out if that is so."
That's why it's important to remember projection.

Fear/egocentricity screams,
"If you stay with this, I will die!"
And that's true, "I" will die.

Its life is your death.
Its death is your life.

Fear has its own identity.
The identity of fear
is separateness.

Fear is the movement
          away from center.
It is the experience
          of being separate.

It is not a position. It is the movement,
the process, of the illusion of separation.
When you're out there, away from
center, fear becomes your identity.

The fearful "I" that feels itself to be
separate,
  has been created,
  has been born,
  will die,
  and is in grave danger.

Everything is a threat to the survival of that illusion of separation. So we move in fear, and we are fear.

Many of the processes of fear are designed to keep us from seeing how fear is the movement to separation.

Fear forces us to spend our lives dealing with it, ostensibly to overcome it.

But that is a trick.

Only fear (the illusion of separation) would want us to work to be unafraid,

precisely because
it is not possible for a self that feels separate from Life to be unafraid!

Here is a trick to make sure "you" (as the illusion of separation) always exist:

decide that you want something that it is not possible to have and then spend your life pursuing that.

SEPARATION (fear)	NO SEPARATION (no fear)
self	Self
isolation	oneness
abandonment	connection
fear	clarity
deprivation	plenty
anger	forgiveness
illusion of control	letting go
suffering	bliss

ADD YOU OWN

Student and Guide: Early Conditioning

Student: I remember being a child on our farm and standing near the rear end of a horse and having no fear of that and someone yanking me back and telling me I should be afraid and never do that again.

Guide: Something important happened because fear and being stupid and being bad somehow got all put together. Fear and self-doubt undermine the desire to learn when adults say to children, "What's the matter with you? Can't you see that's dangerous? You know better than that!" Children believe you when you tell them they should have known better. They're not sure how that works, but they can only trust that you know what you're talking about.

Children are naturally fearless; they are open to the world and to exploring and learning from it. But when they are repeatedly told that something they have done is stupid and foolish, they are humiliated and eventually no longer find new situations interesting. They stop being excited about exploring the unknown because the unknown has become another opportunity to be wrong.

The child has to be shamed into internalizing adult thoughts and feelings. In fact, the child is fine, even after she's been jerked away and told that she's crazy and could have gotten killed. But soon the child accepts that she is stupid and needs to be afraid. But the fear is not of the horse. The fear is of the adult and the adult's reaction.

Suddenly, the person on whom you depend for survival is upset. Something is wrong!

As a child you have no way of knowing what's going on, but you certainly feel the upset. It frightens you. In one second you have gone from everything is fine to everything is wrong! And it seems to be your fault. Something about the horse...you've done something wrong about the horse and it's bad and dangerous.

I suspect that most of that kind of "learning" never got through to us as children. We just lumped wrong, bad, dangerous and upset together and attached them to horse.

What you really needed was somebody to explain how to be around the horse or the hot stove or the lawnmower or the sharp knife or whatever so that you could feel safe and confident as you deal with these things in life instead of being intimidated by them.

HOW TO ADDRESS FEAR

Student and Guide: A Meeting in the City

Student: Tomorrow I have a meeting in the city and I'm taking the train.

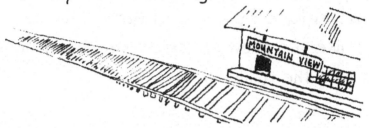

It's been years since I've been to the city, and I have to get from the train station to where the meeting is, which is scary, and I'm also scared about the meeting itself. My whole life I've been afraid of being afraid, of having to go through frightening things alone. So my first reaction was to get somebody to go with me, but that didn't work out. As I have continued to pay attention to this process of fear and self-doubt, I have seen through it. I see it for the fiction it is, and at this point, I'm glad I'm going alone.

It's actually kind of exciting. Tomorrow I'll get on the train alone, go to the city alone, go to the meeting alone. I might even wander around for a while. It's still scary but for the first time it's more like an adventure than a nightmare. I almost feel like the crew on Star Trek, heading off into the unknown.

Guide: That attitude of mind of being present with ourselves is the crux of the matter. It is the experience of not being alone that we've always longed for. If we're present with ourselves, we can drop ideas about doing it right or wrong and learn from it all, just to see what happens, noticing how we react and what we say to ourselves and how it feels and what we do in this or that situation.

Student: There is a part of me who doesn't see this as an adventure at all and is truly terrified. Now and then I hear that voice saying I have a date with a bridge. Before or after the meeting doesn't matter, except that if I jump before I won't have to go through with the meeting.

Guide: The idea is to allow these voices to speak and to turn the attention to them, rather than trying to suppress them. Resisting is the best way to give over all the power to the voices of fear.

Student: Well, there's another part of me saying you shouldn't have to jump off the bridge. Nothing terrible is going to happen. You'll live through this. You've lived through far worse.

Guide: We live our lives trying to avoid imaginary experiences, but the "something terrible" that is going to happen is already happening! It is the process of trying to avoid something terrible happening. It is a projection: there's nothing that's going to happen to us that is worse than living in this kind of fear. *Living in constant fear is as bad as it gets!*

When we drop the idea that we're supposed to be having a different experience and open to the experience we are actually having, we avoid nothing and we fear nothing because we are right here with ourselves.

Fear is the experience of being identified as a separate self.

FEAR and SEPARATENESS are synonyms.

And yet,
    avoiding fear,
    resisting fear,
    fearing fear,
are greater problems than fear.

If we had learned to believe that the sensations we called "happiness" meant that awful things might happen to us, we would now have the same reactions to happiness that we have to fear.

It's not the **experience**,
                it's the **belief!**

We often operate out of beliefs.

Hypothetical Example
-I want my boss not to smoke in meetings. I'm miserable and hate it, but I don't dare say anything. Why? Each time I'm in that situation, a series of beliefs plays out just below my conscious awareness. In this case the series is:
- If I say something, she'll get angry.
- She has a lot of power in my life.
- If she retaliates by firing me, I'd be without work, money, resources, and options.
- I'll be on the street; I'll starve to death or be murdered.
- If I say something to her about not smoking in our meetings, I'll be putting my life in danger.

Realization of non-separation
is the ultimate (and only) "control."

We are desperate to control because we
believe ourselves to be separate, alone,
and vulnerable.
When we are not separate, there is no
one to protect.
We are invincible and can be defenseless.

The way to be invulnerable is to be
completely vulnerable. When there are
no walls or fears or defenses for the
"slings and arrows" to bump up against,
we are invulnerable.

To be open to total vulnerability requires
going beyond fears and knowing that we
have never been separate from True
Nature, from All That Is.

Fear of the unknown

is actually
fear of my imagination.

Many of us see ourselves as victims of fear, as if fear is chasing us through life and we must elude it.

Let's switch this around. Let's become the hunters, and fear, the hunted.

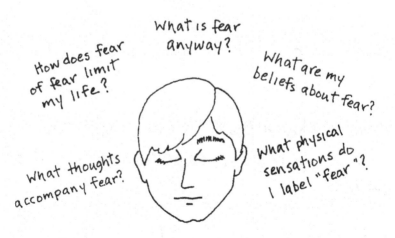

Look to see how fear
is set up in your mind.

Question every fear thought. Learn to ask:

How do I know that? Is that true? Who says so? Is that my **experience** or is it a **belief**?

Is that happening NOW? Is that true NOW?

Learn to explore:
    assumption
    speculation
    rumor
    prejudice
    negativity

Being negative will not keep the things
you don't want to happen from happening.

What if we replace those voices that warn and threaten us...

You're just not quite good enough.

They're going to laugh at your suggestion.

You have no courage. Give up.

You can't do it. Don't even try.

Be careful not to make a mistake!

You don't try hard enough.

You are lazy and boring.

You are too loud! Calm down!

with messages that support our inherent adequacy and our growth toward a fun and free life?

Go ahead. Give it your best shot. It will be okay.

There is nothing wrong with you.

You are kind and generous.

You are never alone. I'll always be with you.

Your feelings are okay whatever they are.

If we are afraid of fear,
we feed it
and it grows.

If we leave fear to itself,
if we give it no power,
          no energy,
          (yes, this is possible!)
eventually it consumes itself.

At the bottom
of the abyss...

BLISS

Becoming a Mentor to Ourselves

Mentor: a wise and trusted counselor
- thefreedictionary.com

**If we can become for ourselves
the Mentor we always wished we had,
everything in life
becomes an exciting adventure.**

We can do the things we always wanted to
do but believed we couldn't. We can live
our lives in the company of someone who
loves us and cares about us and supports
us in our natural eagerness to grow and
natural intelligence about how to do that.

If we look at life
as an opportunity
to end our suffering,
as an opportunity
to embrace and heal
all that has happened to us,

our attention moves
AWAY from trying
to fix ourselves and
figure out everything
and TOWARD being with
ourselves
as we live our daily lives.

So, the critical shift in consciousness in the healing relationship is away from judgment and self-hate and toward the place of compassion from which I can embrace the part of me who's afraid, confused, uncertain, and unskilled.

From the place of compassion, I assist the small part of me who wants to explore and experience and be successful in situations in which I have not had any support, those areas I've never explored because I didn't have anyone to help me through the frightening, difficult, painful places.

FIRST DATE   PEER PRESSURE
FIRST JOB
LEGAL   FIRST   LOST
PROBLEM   HEALTH   CHILD   JOB
CONCERNS
REBELLIOUS   MARITAL   LOSS OF
CHILD   DIFFICULTY   FAITH
ILLNESS   FAILED TO   MONEY
IN FAMILY   QUALIFY   PROBLEMS
SECRETS

Instead of becoming

SMALLER AND SMALLER

as I close my mind and heart against all
that would be threatening or frightening,
my world becomes

LARGER AND LARGER

as I help that small part of me go
forward
into life.

This "small part of me" is also the
spontaneous,
excited,
adventuresome,
brave part—

the one who was there before those
qualities were frightened out of me.

When I approach everything
as an opportunity to heal,
there's nothing that will not be
available to me.

If everything new becomes an
opportunity to open the heart of
compassion and embrace in that
compassion aspects of myself that have
felt timid and insecure and threatened,
then I will rush toward
the new,
the unknown,
the challenging.

I will seek new ways
to bring me back
to myself.

The childlike part of me who was shamed
for not knowing, being awkward, or "doing
things wrong" will be excited to have the
encouragement and support to try new
things.

So, rather than saying to myself,
    "I can't do that,"
    "I'd look foolish,"
    "What would people say?"
    "It would be a waste of time,"

I can decide to give this excited,
enthusiastic part of me all of the life
experiences she never got to have.

        "I can't"
        becomes
        "What now?"

Now I begin to accept opportunities to
meet new people,
learn new sports,
start a business,
speak in public,
build a new house,
travel, write, sing—

pursuing with wild abandon

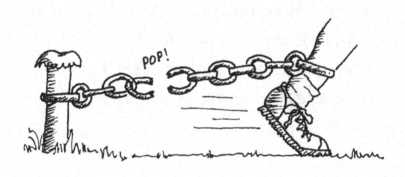

all that brings me closer to who I always
have been.

Because we are most often identified with both the socialized child and the socialized adult within us, we get stuck moving back and forth between a child's fear and an adult's fear.

But it is possible to find within ourselves a way of experiencing life that was ours before we were taught to be afraid, before we were convinced that life is scary and overwhelming, when the world was a place of awe and wonder, when we had boundless energy because there was nothing keeping us from simply being present in the moment.

That's the place we're looking for.

 The only thing that can help us move back to the enthusiasm of the pre-socialized child is to come from the place of compassion within ourselves that can embrace the fear of the frightened child and the socially conditioned fear of the adult.

When we come into that compassionate awareness that is not afraid of the fear, that can embrace the fear, we are able to heal the wounds of the child and the adult and begin to live the lives we have always wanted to live.

Student and Guide: The Dark

Student: I have a friend who is terrified of the dark. In bed at night she hears noises and imagines a burglar is about to kill her. She can't sleep. I wonder how being one's own mentor might work in this instance.

Guide: The best opportunities are the ones we cannot avoid. They are our greatest gift and greatest ally. Without them we would keep putting things off, and procrastination is another one of the ways fear protects itself. "I know I need to look at that, but not right now. I need to be a little stronger." But our own internal mechanisms keep bringing us into the situation. Often we face it only because we no longer have any choice.

And that's regrettable for two reasons. First, at that point it has all become so serious and so grim that we don't see that it can be interesting and fun. Second, it reinforces our inadequacy.

But if we get to the point of saying, "Yes, this is good, I want to see how this works," we are empowered by that. I am no longer a victim waiting around until I have no choice, just fighting for survival and praying I live through it all. I become proactive. In that sense, it's very good to be pushed to our limits so that we can no longer postpone looking at our fear.

If I were your friend who is afraid of the dark, the first thing I would do is make everything just as safe as I need it to be. I would check all the locks on the doors and windows. I would install an alarm system. If I'm afraid to go down the hall to the bathroom in the middle of the night, I'd build a bathroom onto my bedroom, whatever is required. The point is to show the part of me who is afraid that I really am on her side, and she's finally number one with somebody. She might still be afraid, but maybe she won't feel quite so alone.

What to do next? I might ask her to tell me what she's afraid of, and I would write down her thoughts and feelings, being as specific and detailed as possible. I would ask her to tell me the worst that could happen. I would help her make alternative plans. If this happens, we will do that. If you get too scared tonight, we will go to a hotel.

Every step of the way
                    watching what happens.

Student: You're describing the willingness to go to any length...

Guide: Any length, yes, to take care of this frightened child inside of me. That is the relationship that is missing. It has nothing to do with the content. She is experiencing a dramatization of what it  feels like to be abandoned by my "adult" self. In that sense she is already in the hands of a maniac.

Student: So the Mentor would be supporting her through this situation?

Guide: Yes. "Even if somebody comes in and gets us, we would be together. We cannot prevent life, we cannot control events, but I'll be here with you, no matter what." You only have to do this once to begin breaking down the process of abandonment and the fear that follows that.

Student: It doesn't matter what you work with?

Guide: It doesn't matter a fig. The content is irrelevant.

Student: Where does the Mentor come from? If I could do that for myself, I wouldn't have a problem.

Guide: You can do it, and the quickest way to find that out is to realize that you already know what you need to hear. If you're interacting with someone close to you and you want a certain response and you're not getting it, how do you know the response you want?
You know from within yourself.
It exists inside you.

We say to others what we want to hear. So if you are with a small child or an animal that is frightened, what do you say? Do you say it's ok, it's all right, I am here, you are fine?

You already know
how you want to be supported
and loved and cared for.
You can provide that for yourself!

If you pay close attention, you'll see how you stop yourself from receiving the mentoring that is already there.

In receiving there is the experience of
wholeness/oneness/satisfaction.

We focus on DE**PRI**VATION

because it helps us maintain our illusion
of being separate,
of needing to get more of something.*

*We never get it because it constantly
changes!

Once you establish the mentoring relationship with yourself, it feels the way it should have felt in childhood.

You're absolutely safe and cared for and loved and approved of and watched over.

Then you're free to do whatever you want to do because nothing terrible can happen to you. With a sense of safety, you can explore the whole world. Once that mentoring process is in place, you could apply it to anything.

What fear (depression, anger, sadness, etc.) says	What the mentor says

With every fear thought that arises, take a few minutes to do this exercise. It might take a while to find your true mentor, but don't give up. The Mentor hasn't given up on you.

The Process

Let's say I'm terrified of dogs, and I'm going to be desensitized. First, I would look at a dog and then gradually get close to it and eventually touch it and so on. But I'm also afraid of water. And bridges. And heights. And... The point is to acknowledge that the identity being maintained is fear, because once we see how the process of fear works, it has broad application.

But if we focus only on the content, there's no ability to turn to the next thing we're afraid of and apply it to that. If we were just dealing with the fear of elevators, then we would just throw this person in and have them go up and down, up and down until they no longer cared. But that's not what this is about. We're attempting to get to the fear itself.

This is not about heights or dogs or public speaking.

It's about the fear that motivates us and how we maintain it.

Do something you fear,*
not to conquer the fear,
not to accomplish a task,

but to familiarize yourself
with the processes
fear uses to protect itself.

*I encourage you to start with small
fears and then move on to bigger ones.

Never make a contest with conditioning.

If a voice says,
   "I can't, I'm afraid,"

the most helpful kind of response is,
"It's all right to be afraid.
I'm here with you.
We'll take it slowly. It's OK."

And if the voice says,
"But you're just a coward!"

it's helpful not to argue. It doesn't
matter what someone says. Why waste
your time being defensive? Being
whatever and however you are is fine.
And once you have accepted that,
                    the contest ends.

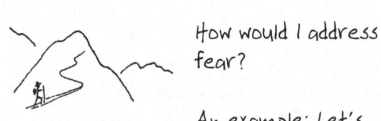

How would I address fear?

An example: Let's say I have a fear of heights. I hate to fly. I won't stay above the second floor in a hotel, I avoid bridges wherever possible, I don't hike in the mountains, etc.

What to do?
First, I learn to disidentify from the part of me who is afraid. Until I disidentify from that part and move into the Mentor role, I'm pretty much incapable of compassionate response.

It is important to note that while I'm identified with the part of me who is afraid, I am most often not actually experiencing the object of my fear.

It's not as if I'm walking over to the edge of the cliff, peering over, and then feeling the sensations of fear in my body.

The mere **idea** of a cliff sends me into a panic. So I avoid cliffs so that I won't be afraid. Am I really afraid of cliffs? Is that what I'm feeling <u>now</u>? No, there aren't any cliffs around. I'm afraid of my feelings. I'm afraid of fear.

ANXIETY

is the fear of fear,
the dread of an experience
I won't be able to stand.

The next step is to make peace with how I'm feeling. For many of us, that notion is revolutionary. We were taught that feelings are something to
get through,
get over with,
get away from,
or deny.

I SHOULD BE OVER THIS BY NOW!

Most feelings are
unsettling,
untrustworthy,
embarrassing,
inconvenient,
even dangerous.

I CAN'T BE SUCCESSFUL IN BUSINESS AND HAVE MY FEELINGS TOO!

So, to make peace with your feelings, imagine that you're simply going to co-exist with them. You don't have to worry about them or control them; you don't even have to take them personally (!!). All you have to do is let the feelings be, and, if you stay with it, before long they will let you just be.

How does that work?

You watch your feelings. You have a front row center seat. You don't have to perform. You're the spectator.

Remember, you have disidentified from the one who's afraid, and you are prepared to be a mentor,
but for now
you're just
watching.

As strange as it might sound,

WE DON'T HAVE TO TAKE OUR FEELINGS PERSONALLY.

It might be helpful to keep a journal of your investigation for a specific fear.

You could write down what your sequence of steps would be: imagining the building, driving there, walking up to the building, getting in the elevator and closing the door, riding up to the top, and then, finally, walking over to the edge and peeping over.

THE ADVENTURES OF JOHN AND THE TEN-STORY BUILDING			
SENSATIONS	THOUGHTS	EMOTIONS	BELIEFS

And with each step you would write down the sensations that arise, the thoughts that go through your head, the emotions that flood your body, and the beliefs you hold about the whole process.

And never take any of it personally.

Now you're ready to address your fear of heights—

not to get over the fear,
not to learn to be all right in high places,
not to change or fix yourself.

**You're doing this to bring
the light of conscious awareness
to the subject of fear.**

You're going to demystify the whole subject of fear.

You're going to learn to be the mentor you always wished you had.

You're going to embrace the part of you who is afraid and has always felt alone and abandoned and unsupported.

Perhaps, at the end of this fascinating journey, you will be relaxed and comfortable at any height.

Perhaps not.

The result is not the point.

Compassionate awareness is the point.

And so you begin. You decide you're going to go to the top of the ten-story building. It might take several stages before you actually go anywhere. Just sitting and thinking about it might be enough to bring up the fear. If so, start there.

You could set up a time each day to work with the fear. Just a few minutes might be enough at the beginning. Do this so that the fear doesn't assault you every time you're not paying attention.

(And notice that is exactly how it happens! You're right there watching, paying close attention, and it's hard to find the fear. Turn your attention away and ZAP! The voices try to scare you to death.)

The procedure is the same each time. You take whatever step would bring up the fear. Perhaps now you drive to the building and sit in your car in the parking lot.

Just be with whatever happens.

You're watching,
seeing ever more subtle levels,
really hearing what the voices are saying,

seeing the belief systems behind the voices, watching your emotions react to the voices, and feeling the sensations.

It becomes so familiar you could map the whole process.

"I do this, then I feel that, and then I say that, and then I feel such and such, and then...."

Not many mysteries left at this point!
It's all pretty predictable stuff!

So, you have become completely familiar with the whole process of fear, and yet the thought of standing looking over the edge of that building still starts the voices shrieking, "I CAN'T!"

That's OK. We're not trying to make it to the edge of the building. We're finding out about the tyrant named fear.

Remember,

this is a spiritual process. When we catch
this little beast, we're not going to
destroy it, we're going to embrace it.

We're going to include it in
acceptance
and compassion.

We're going to love it into extinction.

Student and Guide: The Right/Wrong Trap

Student: I was hoping to come here today and get some answers, but you keep asking us questions, and all I hear you saying is the same old thing: pay attention. I'm disappointed that's what it's about. I want to figure out how to get over the fear, and sitting in meditation doesn't do it for me. I know you're saying there isn't a right way, but I'm convinced there must be.

Guide: The conviction that there is a right way is one of the processes fear uses to protect itself. Since there isn't a "right way," staying stuck is a matter of believing there is, not of seeing the fear. It keeps you looking for the right way instead of looking at what is really going on.

Student: But I don't see what's going on. It sounds exciting when you describe it, but none of that happens when I'm just sitting there, and I get bored.

Guide: It is boring to egocentricity.

Student: I'm getting tired of sitting on the cushion because I don't pay attention most of the time, and this voice keeps telling me I'm doing it wrong.

Guide: What are you doing when you're sitting there?

Student: I'm breathing. I'm trying to see how to disidentify. But really I'm waiting for the meditation period to be over and not paying attention at all.

Guide: What are you paying attention to when you're not paying attention? How do you know you're not paying attention?

Student: I'm thinking of things I need to do when I leave here.

Guide: Ah. So when you're sitting there on the cushion, what you're paying attention to is things you need to do later. And you believe that's doing it wrong because you should be paying attention to something else.

Student: Yes, I should be paying attention to my breathing and the sensations in my body. Isn't that the right way to do it? (general laughter)

Guide: This is really good for all of us because it's the belief that there really is a right way to do it that keeps us from simply being present to what is going on. But we don't see that belief because we are immersed in it.

Student: I do see that I'm caught in a belief because as soon as you said that I thought, okay the right way to do it is that there is no right way to do it.

Guide: It's not that trying to do it right is the wrong way to do it; it's just that trying to do it right keeps us stuck. If we think, "I have to let go of this right/wrong continuum," we're right back on it. Finding ourselves caught in this trap over and over can be really frustrating.

Student: Yes, and then I just feel sick of the whole thing.

Guide: And that frustration keeps us in the same place. What the frustration signals—same with the boredom—is that we're getting perilously close to seeing through all of this. Everything needs to intensify so we will turn our attention to the frustration itself, the boredom itself, the fear itself, whatever is there, and away from the right/wrong trap.

Student: For me it's more like rage than frustration. So should I turn my attention to the rage instead of the right and wrong?

Guide: A short cut, at least intellectually, is to get it that there is nothing wrong with anything. It's the comparisons that keep us stuck. So if you want to know what's going on, turn your attention to that, not comparing it with some other way it should be. When rage is there, turn your attention to rage. When boredom is there, turn your attention to boredom. When frustration is there, turn your attention to frustration.

Student: And when I'm distracted...

Guide: Turn your attention to distraction.

Student: I have this theory that everything in me is fear-based or I wouldn't be so desperate to always figure

out the right way. I think that if fear
weren't driving me, things would just be
okay. But my belief is that without fear, I
would make a big mess of my life.

Guide: Without fear, things would just be
what they are. When we are centered,
nothing is personal and there is no idea of
fault or blame or control over what
happens. The reason
fear keeps such a
tight grip on us is
that we believe
there is a right way
for things to be, and we think that finding
the right way to do everything will protect
us and we won't have to be afraid.

Student: I'm getting excited about this
because I think I'm hearing something
very different in the whole idea of paying
attention. It's not a means to an end,
which is the way I've been thinking about
it—"if I just pay attention, I'll get

answers"—but it is the end itself. I remember you saying that paying attention is freedom. So I'm getting the sense of living in that process rather than getting something out of it.

Guide: Exactly. Well put.

Student: And so the duality comes together, the process and the content, because paying attention to the content becomes process, and the process itself becomes content.

Guide: "The same eyes with which I see God, God sees me."

Worry, fear, and negativity do not stop life from happening.

Situation	Possibility	Possibility	Possibility	Possibility?
There's no point asking for a raise. I know I won't get it.	You ask and do not get a raise.	You ask and do get a raise.	You don't ask and are fired for not being assertive.	
She's in college now, but if I let her have a car she might have an accident.	You get her a car and she has an accident.	You get her a car and she does not have an accident.	You do not get her a car and she has an accident on her bicycle.	
I really want out of our relationship, but if I say anything I'm afraid he'll be hurt.	You say something and he's really hurt.	You don't say anything and live in misery.	You say something and he acts relieved.	

It becomes an adventure to see what happens when I do the thing I fear and when I don't, watching very carefully...

sensations, emotions, thoughts, beliefs, everything about it.

There is a slight little movement and a whole chain of events is activated.
Where does it start?
What do I believe about this?
What happens if I say yes?
What happens if I say no?
What do I think this reveals about me?

I watch myself say, "This is boring. I've seen this so many times," or "I hate this. I don't want to do this." Watching "the same old thing" over and over. And eventually realizing that none of it means anything (and that when we are present nothing is ever "the same old thing.")

Student and Guide: More Right and Wrong

Student: Most of my fear centers on right/wrong also. Will I do it right? How can I be sure it's right? These questions are fueled by endless replays of all the things I've done wrong. Today I was trying to come back to the moment rather than go with these same imaginary scenes from the future and rehashings of the past. The voices would begin to say things like, "If you don't try to do the right thing, if you're not concerned about understanding how life works, you're no different from an animal. You're no different from that bug down there."

Guide: As if one more beating about something that's past or one more rehearsal for a scene that is never going to happen is going to enable you finally to accomplish the impossible: to know how something is going to turn out before it happens. The ultimate illusion of control.

Once again, if I came up to you and began recounting all of the most difficult periods of your life, pointing out how you could have done this or you should have done that or if only you had thought of that, and then if I began coaching you on all the ways you should approach your life in the future, what would your response be?

Would you think
I liked you,
cared about you,
had your best interests at heart?

I hope not. I hope you would wonder what my game was. What on earth would motivate me to want you to feel bad about yourself? Could it possibly be a way of gaining power over you? A way of having control over you? Very likely.

So, the next time that voice starts trying to convince you that you should leave the peace and comfort of the present moment to wander around with it in the world of possible future calamities, you might just give it a polite "no, thank you" and invite it to come sit quietly here in the safety of this moment with you.

Fear of making a mistake...

From center
there is no such thing as a mistake.
From off center
(illusion of separation)

**almost everything we
do, feel, say, and achieve
should be
different and better
than it is.**

"I'm always in a hurry. It feels like everything is urgent. I must work and move as fast as possible or I won't get everything done and something bad will happen."

The important thing is **to be with the urgency.** Instead of letting it dictate what you're going to do to satisfy it, turn your attention around and focus directly on urgency.

Ask urgency the same questions you would ask boredom and frustration.

Student and Guide: Speaking in Public

Student: For years I have struggled with speaking in front of groups. I can force myself to do it, but the problem persists. I observe and observe that fear, but I feel like I could observe forever and it would make no difference.

Guide: If the relationship to fear does not change, it's a clue that we are not observing what needs to be observed. It's like watching the magician's hands and missing what's really happening.

Also, as long as we're expecting a particular outcome, it doesn't work. It won't work to observe the part of me who fears speaking in groups if my motivation is to stop being that way. What I need to know is the *process* that is at work here. Then it won't matter whether I speak or not.

Generally, when someone has trouble speaking it's because there was some sort of trauma. Children tend to be naturally expressive until something stops them. So my guess is that there is a part of you who was traumatized and that trauma has been covered over.

What we are doing is seeing how fear protects itself. Surrounding our identity are layers of protection, and we're removing them so we can see how it all works. If you continue to be uncomfortable talking that doesn't mean something is wrong, it just means you haven't seen what there is to see.

Student: What if I never see it?

Guide: The part of you asking that hopes you never will. Let's say you had a child who was kidnapped from your house. You devote your life to finding this child. Someone says, "What if you never find the child?" Wouldn't your response be something like, "What is the point of such a question? I'm not going to quit looking just because I might not find my child. Clearly my chances are better if I keep looking."

It's not that your life is a failure if you don't find the child or a success if you do. You're just looking because the child is missing and finding the child is what you're trying to do. So in the same way, you are looking simply because you are looking.

Student: I'm wondering if it would be good to try to force myself...

Guide: When you have observed the processes involved enough to know what is really going on—what happens physiologically, emotionally, mentally, behaviorally—and you are present to yourself in that situation, you will have given that part of yourself enough freedom that he will speak spontaneously. You are providing a safe environment for him so that when he expresses himself, he just expresses himself.

We can break out of the cycle of suffering by being for ourselves what was missing when we were children: someone to listen and be there with us as we struggle, someone who accepts us no matter what.

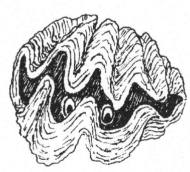 We need to stop taking ourselves personally. We need to see that we are simply human beings, and this is what happens to human beings, this is how human beings operate. We come into the world with the ability to experience

ourselves as separate. Our own particular experience of being separate from all that is, the "what" of it, the content, is just another typical little story except to ourselves.

"I grew up with these people and they did this to me and then that happened and I tried to cope but it didn't work and I became a victim to that..."

We can each plug in our own story about how it was. But it's so difficult to stand back enough from the content to see the process.

Once I see that this
is just the process of
being a human being,

I have a chance
of not taking it all
so personally.

I didn't create this,
I was born into it,
so why should I spend my life being
punished for being human?

Punishment
is another process
with which fear protects itself.

As long as I'm caught in believing
that this is right
and that is wrong
and this makes me a good person
and that makes me a bad person,
I'm completely enmeshed in egocentricity.

Once I realize that this is a waste of time
and that duality, the world of opposites, is
simply a way of staying stuck in suffering,
I have a chance of stepping back, of
disidentifying enough to get out of that
system, of not taking myself personally.
Now I can observe how a human being
operates and see what's going on.

Now I have a chance of being a
compassionate mentor for myself. There
is motivation to move into that place to
end suffering, to help all beings.

The fastest way to stay identified is to
believe the voices in our head:

I don't understand.
That doesn't make sense.
What about this?
What if this happens?
I need to be careful of that.

Worrying that something terrible might happen prevents me from noticing what is already happening, which is that I am actively maintaining the fear that is stifling me! It's projection at work again: the very system I'm projecting out onto other people is the system that is operating me.

I'm the one who maintains this, and then I am a victim to it.

The Ski Slope: Mentoring Myself

I took up downhill skiing to celebrate my entrance into the sixth decade of my life.

I had many motivations, one of the primary ones being a commitment to continuing to do new and potentially scary or dangerous things. I do this for all the reasons suggested in this book, and because I work with people on things that are very scary to them but are no longer scary to me. I don't want to lose touch with being scared because it would be too easy to forget what it is like to feel threatened. Becoming an "expert" can make us insensitive to those who don't yet have that

I'm always depressed.

get over it.

expertise, and we can forget that we're an expert only in our one little area.

Being a nervous beginner can keep the compassion and humility exercised.

My first time out on the slope was with a friend who, though not a skier, is an extraordinary athlete. During the course of the day I wound up in some places I should not have been in. I took some bad falls and generally hurt myself a lot. I decided lessons were in order. With lessons, I improved until I could do well enough to have a good time.

One day I was skiing with a friend, and my old ski instructor made me a gift of a lesson with the head instructor at the ski area. "You'll improve dramatically," she assured me. "You're ready for the next level."

In fact, I felt no need to improve dramatically, but it was such a generous offer I overrode that little sense of discomfort that arose with the gift.

It was a disaster. We went high up to a slope that was in deep shade and was quite icy. I was told not to worry about what I had been doing previously, just follow him. Three or four falls later I thanked him and told him the lesson was over and that I was going to get down off that mountain the best way I could. It was a hard thing to say since it wasn't his fault. I didn't want him to feel bad, I just wanted to get me out of there in one piece. The biggest struggle was not succumbing to the voices who wanted to blame me for not listening to myself when I knew I didn't want a lesson in the first place. I suspected that was the end of skiing for me.

Then, a week or so later, my grandson had a vacation day and wanted to ski. He was nine years old and had skied less than I, so I figured I could probably manage.

To prepare, I gave myself absolute permission to do whatever I needed. If I wanted to snowplow all day (a beginner's tactic), I would. If Brian wanted to  go where I couldn't, I'd find an instructor to take him. Every second I was mentoring myself. "It's okay. If you don't like it, you can quit. You don't have to do anything you don't want to do. You never have to ski again if you don't want to. We'll do whatever you'd like."

It was the best day of skiing I've ever had.

I skied more and better than ever before.

The secret is to disidentify.
This all comes down to not allowing
egocentricity to be in charge.

First we watch how we
get hooked back
into the fear.

Next we watch
the process of identification as it
happens.

Instead of sitting in the audience and
watching the magic show and wondering
how it's all done, I'm sitting in the front
row waiting for the magician to come on
stage, and I'm looking closely at
everything. Because I'm leading this
investigation. I'm not a victim in this. I'm
the pursuer. I can get up on the stage,
go around behind the magician and look in
from the wings. No vantage point is
forbidden to me.

I will probably have to go back to that
show again and again, and I will probably
get to see how I get distracted from my
pursuit, how my attention goes
elsewhere, but my aim is to see
            every
                single
                        thing
                            that
                                happens.

I'm not doing this for any reason other
than wanting to know how it all works.

It's not going to make me a better
person.

It's not going to get rid of anything for
me.

        That's not the point.

The point is that now I'm in a different
relationship with the fear.

I am bringing the light
of conscious compassionate awareness
to the exploration
of the process of fear.

The continent of fear, of egocentricity, is out there (in there?) for you to explore.

When you start out, it's as if nobody has ever been there before, and as the first explorer you can feel a real thrill.

Being an explorer is not the same as being a traveler. You are not doing this to get from point A to point Z You are doing this for the sake of exploration. You just want to find out everything that is out there in that unknown ~~terror-tory~~ territory.

If you keep at it, you will know every tree, every rock, every turn in the path because you will have gone over every inch of it, back and forth, many times.

If someone else shows up, you will be able to give them directions, although, of course, we would hope that others would want to see it all for themselves.

You can tell them that over there is this interesting feature and across there is something no one would want to miss and once you get to this place it's easier to move on to that place and the trip up this mountain is long and arduous but definitely worth it. This is the attitude we bring to the exploration, not "I've got to get to the other side as quickly and painlessly as possible and every time I take a wrong step it's a mistake."

It has to be seen
        as a great adventure.

I don't know a more effective way to be with fear than to be still with it in compassionate awareness.

For me, compassionate awareness is most simply experienced in a meditation practice.

A period of solitude and silence each day helps us to realize that
    silence,
    stillness,
    and compassion

are who we truly are, are our True Nature, and that compassion
                is far greater
            and more powerful
                than fear.

If I want to be free,
I must find the courage
and the willingness
to be still

and face the fear that arises
when I attempt to come back
to my Self.

FACING FEAR
WITH
COMPASSION:

RECORDING
AND
LISTENING
PRACTICE

Here is a seven-part conversation, the first six parts of which are followed by Recording and Listening (R/L for short) exercises for moving through any fear.

Recording and Listening is one of the most powerful, transformative ways of directly accessing the wisdom, love, and compassion that is our Authentic Nature. It is the most effective way we've found to learn to direct the attention.

It is based on a radical idea that we can live in a conversation about what is true, what is real, and what is arising in life in the moment instead of with the voices of egocentric karmic conditioning/self-hate. If intelligence, love, and compassion is what we are (we use the singular "is" because we see intelligence, love, and compassion as one thing), would it not have something vital to say?

For in-depth instruction and many inspiring testimonials, visit recordingandlistening.org.

Our book *What Universe Are You Creating?* includes a fun set of games to develop an R/L practice.

Should you run into resistance with R/L, read *I Don't Want To, I Don't Feel Like It: How Resistance Controls Your Life and What to Do about It.*

One

Student: I am hoping you can help me with my fear.

Guide: Well, as perhaps you know, fear is a set of sensations in the body that have been given the label "fear" and have a fearful story attached to them.

Student: Are you saying fear isn't real?

Guide: We are conditioned to believe many things are real that are nothing more than a combination of unexamined beliefs and assumptions. We believe there is a thing that is "fear," but when we break it down we realize that without a label and a story the sensations could be anything and that sensations themselves have no inherent meaning. So, what fear are you looking at?

Student: I have to give a presentation but I am terrified to speak in public.

Guide: Tell me about being terrified.

Student: Oh, I just panic. My brain goes crazy. I can't think of anything or remember anything. My heart pounds. I sweat. My hands shake. I feel sick. I'm a mess. My brain screams, "I don't want to do this!"

Guide: Very good. You are certainly in touch with the sensations, the labels, and the story.

Student: But that's not going to get me through the presentation.

Guide: But that clarity will take you a long way in the right direction. So pick up your recorder and record what it feels like to be terrified and what you are told it means.

Recording and Listening Exercise

What fear do you want to work with? Turn on the recorder and record what the sensations in your body are, what story you hear inside your head, and what you are told it means to "be afraid."

Two

Student: I made the recording.

Guide: How was that?

Student: I felt terrified.

Guide: Very good. Now what I would like you to do is to sit quietly for a few minutes, just breathing and relaxing and letting yourself get here. And then, when you feel ready, turn on the recorder and listen to that person caught in that fear. Listen as if you are listening to a wonderful person you love dearly expressing their fear.

Student (later): I did that. I listened.

Guide: How was that?

Student: It was sad. I felt really sorry that someone should be that afraid.

Guide: It is sad, isn't it? Do you want to help that person out?

Student: Yes.

Guide: This is very good. Because we must first move from being the one who is afraid to being the one who can assist the one who is afraid.

Recording and Listening Exercise

Sit quietly, breathe, and relax. When you are ready, listen to the recording you made. Move from being the one who is afraid to the sympathetic observer who can assist the one who is afraid.

Three

Guide: Do you have a sense of how the fear begins?

Student: All I have to do is think about the presentation and I feel the first tremors.

Guide: Ok. Go on and imagine yourself giving the presentation.... Everyone is looking at you.... Are you feeling the sensations?

Student: Oh yes!

Guide: Is there anything about those sensations, those tremors, that mean you can't do a good job of giving your presentation?

Student (laughs): No, not really. They feel kind of like fluttery butterflies, but I can sort of see that they are not actually scary.

Guide: So, turn on your recorder and record the insight that the sensations feel fluttery and like butterflies, but there is nothing scary about the sensations themselves.

Recording and Listening Exercise

Imagine facing the situation you have identified as frightening. Picture it as clearly as you can and feel the sensations in your body. Where do you feel them? How would you describe them? Is there anything inherently scary about the sensations? Do the sensations mean you should be afraid? Do they mean you are in danger?

Record any insights or realizations you have seen in this exercise.

Four

Student: I can see the sensations are not scary, but it feels like I'm going to die.

Guide: That's why we want to do this bit by bit because the conditioned story is the equivalent of "I am going to do the presentation, it will be horrible, and I will feel awful." And the story ends there. The implication is that you will be humiliated, you will fail, you will be judged, and that will be the end of you. You'll never recover. Which is silly but that's the unexamined belief.

Guide: Right. I never questioned that.

Recording and Listening Exercise

What is the story implying will happen to you if you proceed? Record it this way: "The story implies that I will...."

Five

Student: So, are you saying the voices only claim they will protect me from being in a horrible situation where I'll fail and be humiliated but that's not really what they're doing?

Guide: Yes. The worst thing that could happen for those voices telling that fear story is for you to do that presentation and be a smashing success. The fear tactics are meant to *control* you. Fear controls people.

Student: But that doesn't make sense!

Guide: Not until you realize that the voices are interested only in their own survival, not in yours. If you were able to do anything you choose fearlessly, excitedly, and happily would there be any room in your life for those negative, fear-mongering voices?

Student: Hmm, I guess not. So how do I get rid of those voices?

Guide: Getting rid of those voices would be difficult, if not impossible. Fortunately, it is much easier than that. We learn simply to ignore them.

Student (eagerly): How do I do that?

Guide: Remember, you were able to step back from *being* the frightened person to *observing* the frightened person. This is your first step. Next, being able to see, sympathize with, and support someone who is frightened enables you to comfort and reassure that person when the voices begin to instigate fear. Listen again to the person who is afraid. Turn on the recorder and begin to offer the person what is so, what is true. For instance, "It's ok. Everything is all right. Just breathe. Smile at the butterflies. Those sensations in the body don't mean anything. Just keep breathing. Relax. I'm right here. You are not alone. I will be with you no matter what."

Recording and Listening Exercise

Listen to your recording of the person who is caught in fear. Then switch on the recorder and offer that person the support and encouragement they need.

Six

Student: Are you sure this is going to work?

Guide: Yes, and there is a specific reason it works. When you are identified with the frightened person the whole world is that fear, and your reality is being orchestrated by those voices and that story. When you step back and become the conscious compassionate awareness that can support the frightened person, you are no longer afraid.

Student: So I don't need to take classes in giving presentations?

Guide: Correct.

Student: Will this work with everything I am afraid of?

Guide: Yes, because **what we are learning is to direct the attention.** We are taking the attention away from fear. And whatever we take attention from ceases to exist for us. Conversely, what we give attention to grows. For this reason we want to give attention to the moment, the present, this, here, now.

Recording and Listening Exercise

To get a taste of directing the attention, record what you are grateful for in your life right now. Be specific, descriptive, and effusive. Record not just a list, but what you love, what is beautiful, what you care about, what makes you smile in your life that brings you to gratitude.

Notice how making this recording and listening to it transforms your experience.

Seven

Student: So it seems that if I am focused on gratitude I feel gratitude. If I am focused on fear I feel afraid. So the practice is to break the habit of listening to the story of fear.

Guide: Yes. You are breaking the unconscious habit of giving attention to the voices. Any time you become aware of the voices attempting to pull you into a conversation, listen to the recording that brings you back to what is so for you. Each time you hear the story or feel the sensations you were conditioned to call fear, listen to the supportive, encouraging recording you made for the frightened person.

Student: So the content of the recording is not really the point. It's that I am learning to put the attention on now.

Guide: Exactly so. The quality of your life is determined by the focus of your attention.

The following are
Recording and Listening
exercises
for recognizing
fearful conversations
and directing attention
to the peace and joy
of the present.

Situation

It's the end of the month and there are bills that have to be paid. You've put it off longer than you should have. You hate paying bills, are not good with numbers, always make mistakes, and it's just going to be more bad news. You're filled with dread and feel overwhelmed. You don't know where to begin.

Record the steps involved in paying the bills, what precisely needs to happen. Talk yourself through the process as a way of dispelling the unease that comes with the conditioned conversation "it'll be awful." As you speak into the recorder, identify the first, most manageable action you can take. Then turn off the recorder and take that action. If you need to listen to the recording again to determine the next steps, do that. Continue in this way until the project is completed. When the bills are paid, make another recording to congratulate and celebrate the person who successfully overcame overwhelm.

Focus of Attention: Moving from the imaginary to real

Situation

You're about to meet your future mother-in-law for lunch and you're really nervous. You want more than anything to make a good impression so that she will like and approve of you.

Make a recording that reminds you that what you choose is love—for yourself and for this person who is going to be very important in your life. How do you want to be in this relationship? How do you want her to feel? How can you let her know you care about her and are interested in her? Remind yourself that by being present and authentically who you are, you invite her to do the same.

Focus of attention: How you choose to be

Situation

You're engaged with someone in an activity that requires you to make a call to that person, and the conversation in your head is about how you're intruding on them, that you will be putting them in an uncomfortable situation, they won't want to talk to you, they will say something you don't want to hear. That you haven't heard from them means they don't want to engage with you but can't say so. You are afraid of being rejected, but you still have to make the call.

Make a recording that reminds you that **you don't know** what's going on with the other person. Everything you hear about what's going to happen is occurring inside your head. Whatever they say or do, you can choose how you want to be. Perhaps you choose kindness and to trust that we are all adequate to our life experience. Remind yourself that you don't need to take personally anything anyone is doing or saying. You can handle anything that comes your way, and the proof is that you always have!

Focus of attention: There is nothing wrong.

Situation

There's a performance, a play, a tournament, a competition, a presentation. You are eager and excited to do this. You've worked hard and gotten good at this. The voices are predicting failure, humiliation, and defeat. "You'll forget your lines." "You won't play well." "You won't know the answer." "You'll make a fool of yourself."

Make a recording about what you love and enjoy about the activity. Be detailed and specific. What exactly do you relish? What are your favorite parts? How do you feel when you're doing this activity you love? Recall the moments that illustrate your joy in wholeheartedly participating in this thing you love.

Focus of attention: Love and enjoyment

Situation

You have a trip coming up, driving or flying, and the voices start their fear-mongering conversation of dismemberment and death. Images are offered of every awful thing that could possibly happen.

 Make a recording that reassures the one listening to the horror stories that they're not alone. They don't have to go through this difficult experience without support and assistance. "We can't know what might happen, but I'll be with you no matter what. You won't be alone. We'll be together. We can't control the future, but together we can face anything."

Focus of attention: Reassurance

Situation

Everything is fine right now; there's nothing wrong. Then, you see a headline about the state of the economy. Your stomach goes into a knot. What if I lose my job or get sick and can't work? What if I don't have enough saved? I'm not good with money. I don't know what to do. I could wind up homeless.

Make a recording that focuses on appreciation and gratitude for what you have and have always had. Remind yourself that you've always been okay. There's no reason to believe that will change. You're resourceful, capable, skilled, and competent. Make a list of the ways you've been cared for, the people in your life who assist and support you, the resources you have access to. Add a reminder that the only way to be all right in the future is to be all right in the present, and that worry about the future only keeps us from taking whatever action we can take now.

Focus of Attention: Gratitude, Appreciation and Adequacy

Situation

It's 3:00 a.m. and you're awake, mind racing, gripped by terror. You scramble to find the source. Did you hear a noise; is this a premonition of some hideous event; did you have a nightmare?

Make a recording of what is true right now—there's nothing wrong, you're safe in this moment. Encourage yourself to breathe slowly and deeply, feeling the tension leave your body with each breath. Guide yourself to relax the body, beginning with the tips of the toes and moving slowly up through each part of the body, consciously relaxing each part as you go.

Focus of Attention: Calming the body

Note: If this is a recurring experience, you might make a recording before you go to sleep so that it's available when you wake up in terror. You could also make a comforting, reassuring recording you have on loop that plays throughout the night. These can be anything you enjoy listening to—poems, lullabies, quotes, and such.

Situation

You're facing an encounter with an authority—a meeting with the boss, a letter announcing a tax audit, a performance review—a situation in which you are vulnerable and without control.

Make a recording that reminds you that you have no information about what's going to happen in the future and that the voices are talking about consequences that may very well never happen. Focus attention on what's happening right now, reminding yourself to be present and that being present is the best preparation for dealing with anything. Each time attention wanders to the story, gently bring it back to thisherenow, to the breath, to the colors around you, to the sounds you hear, your feet on the ground, etc.

Focus of attention: Getting to the present

Situation

You're visiting relatives and the dynamics are generally stressful and upsetting. There's bound to be conflict. It gets unpleasant. People say hurtful, insensitive things to one another. You'd rather not go but feel you have to. The conversation in conditioned mind reviewing past visits and predicting future catastrophes has you in a state of trepidation.

Make a recording that enables you to drop the stories and return to the present. What is there to enjoy where you are? What's beautiful? When you're here rather than in the stories, record the good things you've received, what you appreciate about your family, good times you've had, laughter, moments of connection.

Focus of the attention: What's working instead of what's not working

Some final thoughts

"Fear" and its synonyms—anxiety, nervousness, agitation, dread, terror, trepidation—are always products of a conversation in conditioned mind. But because we are trained to look to conditioned mind for what is true, and we believe that "I am thinking these thoughts," we assume fear is a true experience and that the fear is real.

As we pay attention, we realize that "I" am not the author of this story. I am listening to a story I am being told.

And so your final R/L assignment is a reminder to recognize the conversation for what it is: a set of unexamined beliefs and assumptions designed to produce sensations in the body that support and maintain the illusion that an imaginary, generated experience is true.

Fear is a process,
a recognizable series of steps.

The antidote to fear
is presence.

The primary technique
for dealing with fear
is to move from being the one
who is afraid
to being the one
who can assist the one
who is afraid.

Work with Cheri Huber

To talk with Cheri call in to Open Air, her internet-based radio show. Archives of the show and instructions on how to participate are available at www.openairwithcherihuber.org.

To work with Cheri on an individual basis, sign up for her email classes at livingcompassion.org/schedule.

Visit www.recordingandlistening.org to learn about Recording and Listening, the practice that is Cheri's passion.

Visit cherihuber.com to access Cheri's latest interviews.

Cheri's books are available from your local independent bookstore, www.keepitsimple.org, and other online booksellers.

A Center for the Practice
of Zen Buddhist Meditation

Visit livingcompassion.org for more
information on Zen Awareness Practice
and the teachings of Cheri Huber.

- Find a schedule of retreats and
  workshops
- Find out more about virtual practice
  opportunities such as Reflective
  Listening, Virtual Meditation and
  Email Classes
- Access newsletters and blogs on
  Zen Awareness Practice
- Sign up for Recording and Listening
  Training
- Find out about our work in a
  community in Zambia. Read blogs
  with updates.

Contact
information@livingcompassion.org

There Is Nothing Wrong with You

An Extraordinary Eight-Day
Retreat based on the book
*There Is Nothing Wrong with You:
Going Beyond Self-Hate*
by Cheri Huber

Inside each of us is a "persistent voice of discontent." It is constantly critical of life, the world, and almost everything we say and do. As children, in order to survive we learned to listen to this voice and believe what it says.

This retreat is eight days of looking directly at how we are rejected and punished by the voices of self-hate and discovering how to let that go. Through a variety of exercises and periods of group processing, participants gain a clearer perspective on how they live their lives and on how to find compassion for themselves and others.

This work is challenging, joyous, fulfilling, scary, courageous, demanding, freeing, loving, kind, and compassionate—compassionate toward yourself and everyone you will ever know.

For information on attending, contact:
information@livingcompassion.org

What Universe Are You Creating? is a playful, powerful way to learn the skill of Recording and Listening, a revolutionary tool for practicing turning attention from incessant, haranguing, karmically conditioned patterns of thought and action to the peace of presence. Recording in your own voice and then listening to kind words, encouragement, inspirational readings, favorite songs, gratitude lists, meditations—in short, being your own Mentor—turns attention away from the constant stream of negative self-talk, robbing it of its power by revealing its illusory nature. ISBN: 9780991596300